“With diverse perspectives, beautiful artwork, and Scripture throughout, this small group study *Migration* is an excellent resource for Christians seeking to understand the global phenomenon of migration.”
**Matthew Soerens,** vice president of advocacy and policy at World Relief and coauthor with Jenny Yang of *Welcoming the Stranger*

“Resources made by and for people of color who are looking to grow in contemplative Christian practices are few and far between, but Made for Pax is an oasis in a spiritual desert. Their commitment to empowering and raising up voices as part of the global majority is a testament to their shalom-filled activism. The Made for Pax Bible Studies are thoughtful resources for folks who are passionate about fostering the flourishing of all.”
**Jenai Auman,** writer and author of *Othered*

“We long for integrity—in ourselves, in society, in the church. I love how the Made for Pax Bible Studies embody integrity in both what they present and how they present it. Addressing important topics often neglected by the church, these books call us to live out a holistic faith—and do so by engaging us holistically as readers. Here are pages filled with poems, prayers, visual art, embodied practices, and more, inviting us to join Jesus step by step, breath by breath, in the work of cultivating integrity and shalom in ourselves and in the world.”
**Michael Stalcup,** poet

“The Made for Pax Bible Study Series is a gift for anyone seeking contemplative scriptural learning. These well-structured studies offer engaging writing and thoughtfully chosen topics. The units on mental health and migration are particularly timely and important, addressing crucial contemporary issues. This is a valuable resource for those seeking deeper understanding, centering often decentered voices.”
**Guesnerth Josué Perea,** director of Black Lives and Contemplation for the Community of the Incarnation

“Migration touches all our lives, whether we realize it or not. Still, it’s a topic too often informed by political pundits rather than Scripture. This study offers an invitation to listen, reflect, and grow with unique, artistic expressions that open fresh conversations.”
**Sarah Quezada,** author of *Love Undocumented*

# MIGRATION

## Experiencing God's Care for Immigrants

**A 6-WEEK INTERACTIVE BIBLE STUDY**

**ALEXIS BUSETTI AND DORCAS CHENG-TOZUN**

An imprint of InterVarsity Press
Downers Grove, Illinois

InterVarsity Press
P.O. Box 1400 | Downers Grove, IL 60515-1426
ivpress.com | email@ivpress.com



Written by Alexis Busetti and Dorcas Cheng-Tozun



InterVarsity Press® is the publishing division of InterVarsity Christian Fellowship/USA®. For more information, visit intervarsity.org.



While any stories in this book are true, some names and identifying information may have been changed to protect the privacy of individuals.

Published in association with Joy Eggerichs Reed of Punchline Agency.

The publisher cannot verify the accuracy or functionality of website URLs used in this book beyond the date of publication.

Cover design: Faceout Studio
Interior design: Nat Maxey
Cover images: © CSA-Printstock / DigitalVision Vectors and © CSA Images via Getty Images
Interior images: Made for Pax

ISBN 978-1-5140-1292-5 (print)
ISBN 978-1-5140-1293-2 (digital)

Printed in the United States of America ♾

**Library of Congress Cataloging-in-Publication Data**
A catalog record for this book is available from the Library of Congress.

30 29 28 27 26 25 | 8 7 6 5 4 3 2 1

# CONTENTS


Welcome 01

How to Use This Study 03

Session 1: Opening 07

Session 2: Manifesto 15

Session 3: Myth 29

Session 4: Material 43

Session 5: Motion 55

Session 6: Closing 67

Additional Resources 78

Notes 80

Journaling Pages 81

# Welcome

Welcome to this six-week study on migration!

This course takes you on a deep exploration of how migration honors God and forms us to become more like Jesus. By the time you complete all six sessions of this study on migration, you will: (1) gain an understanding of the centrality of migration to the human experience, including the biblical narrative; (2) understand the myths that try to recast migration as a threat, and the individual and societal harm that results; and (3) learn how God calls us to develop the heart of a migrant in our faith and our lives.

Migration is a key topic that young Christians want to know about yet are challenged to find relevant, thoughtful, biblically based resources that answer their questions. This study includes a diverse collection of Jesus-centered art, scholarship, and storytelling, primarily created by people of color, that provides teaching, guidance, and opportunities for reflection. In addition to studying Scripture, you will also read essays and personal testimonies, experience spoken word and poetry, meditate on visual art, and listen to or watch in-depth interviews and panels. We hope you will experience a spiritual feast for your senses and your soul, inspiring you in your journey to learn more about the character of God and the discipleship he calls each of us to.

*Migrant Covenant*
BY URIAS ABRAHAM

# HOW TO USE THIS STUDY

Below is a breakdown of the study structure and approach. The opening and closing sessions are distinct from the middle four sessions and have less content to allow for more discussion and reflection. In each session, you will also engage with unique audio and video content. Scan the accompanying QR code on each page to access the digital material.

| | | |
|---|---|---|
| **Session 1** | Opening | Introduces the topic of migration and creates space to reflect on initial ideas, teachings, questions, and doubts. |
| **Session 2** | Manifesto | Overviews the differing perspectives on migration and explores the foundational spiritual truth that guides the rest of the sessions. |
| **Session 3** | Myth | Names and deconstructs common false beliefs and teachings about migration within church and society. |
| **Session 4** | Material | Delves into Jesus-centered, biblically based teachings on migration and its implications for how we live. |
| **Session 5** | Motion | Explores meaningful ways to embrace relevant embodied practices in our everyday lives. |
| **Session 6** | Closing | Reviews the main themes from the study and facilitates next steps to apply learnings in practical and meaningful ways. |

## Opening Session

The Opening session begins with (1) a pulse check to gauge where participants are coming from at the start of the study, followed by (2) an introduction to the overall study. Then you will engage (3) a short recorded personal story and (4) the four path point statements, or the overarching themes of the study, along with a holy imagination exercise, before closing with (5) a benediction and (6) an application activity.

## Sessions 2–5

You will (1) preview the focus for the week and (2) read the path point statement and a brief reflection that frames the content of the session. Then you will study (3) a passage of Scripture and (4) additional content from a relevant expert. Each session concludes with (5) a communal benediction and (6) an application activity for the week to encourage further learning and embodied action.

## Closing Session

The Closing session provides (1) a review of the content in the entire study and gives space to (2) revisit and reflect upon the path point statements previously studied. Then, you will (3) research the demographics of the immigrants in your community, and (4) come up with practical ways to extend love and care to the migrants around you. You will end your time together with (5) a prayer and benediction.

# OUR DISCIPLESHIP PATHWAY

The four path points of the discipleship pathway—Manifesto, Myth, Material, and Motion—help us unpack one big idea from concept to call to action. These path points are the stepping stones that guide your journey with Jesus, God's Spirit, and each other as we consider how peacemaking impacts our approach to migration.

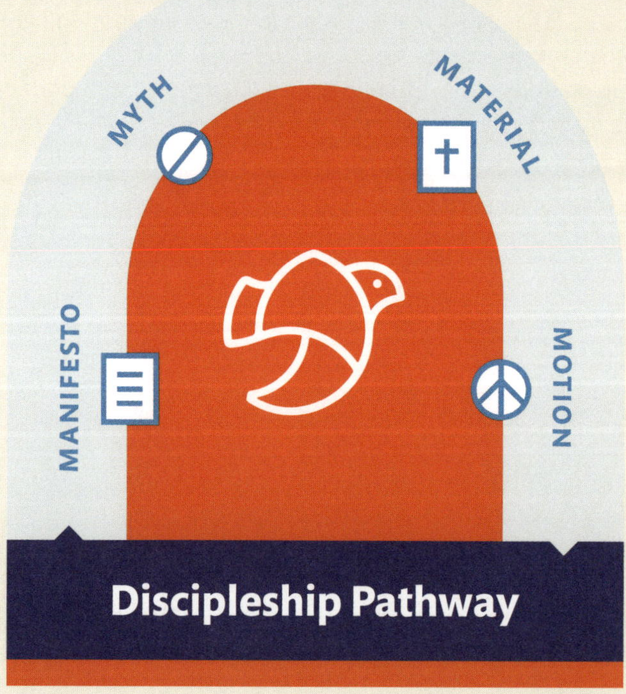

**MANIFESTO—Declaration of Peace**

Proclaim the good news of peace in the world.

**MYTH—Distortion of Peace**

Discern the lies and false narratives that surround us.

**MATERIAL—Expressions of Peace**

Reveal the scriptural witness of peace in the world.

**MOTION—Embodiment of Peace**

Participate in the active work of peace in the world.

# SESSION 1 Opening

We're so glad you have chosen to participate in this six-week study on how migration leads to transformation!

In this first session, we will learn about migration—what it is and how it relates to each of us, regardless of whether or not we have personally migrated. We'll spend time reflecting on our own views of migration, and listening to a personal story of migration. We'll also introduce the path point statements (which are like thesis statements) that we will focus on throughout the study. This session sets up the framework through which we will view the topic of migration.

**Migration** /mī-ˈgrā-shən/ (noun): the act, process, or an instance of moving from one country, place, or locality to another.

## REFLECTION

*As we begin to consider the topic of migration, take about fifteen minutes to consider the following reflection questions.*

1. How does the topic of migration intersect with your own family story or history?

2. When you think of migration, what are the first associations that come to mind? What kind of people do you think of as migrants and immigrants?

3. How do you think God sees migration and the people who undergo migration?

# INTRODUCTION

Throughout human history, people have been on the move. Scripture is filled with stories of individuals, families, and entire communities moving to a new place in response to God's call and provision—and being praised for their faith and obedience. Jesus himself often moved around in response to opportunities, threats, and the desire to connect with new people.

Today, migration is rarely seen through the lens of faith but is instead inserted into debates about politics, economics, security, and national identity. No matter our background, it can be easy to look at some (or all) immigrants suspiciously. We may wonder if they will compete with us for resources and opportunities. We may wonder if they will change our communities in drastic ways.

But the story of God, as recorded in the Bible, almost always centers on the story of the migrant. God *loves* migrants, *calls* migrants, is *with* migrants. He asks those of us who are not migrants to extend love, hospitality, and generosity to our migrant brothers and sisters. The heart of God is very much built into the migrant experience.

# PERSONAL STORY

Every story of migration is different, and the more stories we hear, the more we are able to expand our hearts for the experiences of migrants. Josué Carballo-Huertas migrated with his family from Costa Rica to the United States and he shares about the challenges of leaving a home he loved.

*Listen to his story. Then, consider the following reflection questions.*

## "Leaving the Costa Rican Dream"

BY JOSUÉ CARBALLO-HUERTAS

(from "In Their Own Words: Migration Stories from Around the World")

## REFLECTION

1. What is your initial response to Josué Carballo-Huertas's story?

2. For most immigrants, leaving their home country and going someplace new is a complex emotional experience. What are the emotions that Carballo-Huertas expresses? How might God work through such multifaceted, weighty experiences?

# PATH POINT STATEMENTS

Each step in our discipleship pathway has a statement that captures the main idea of that path point. We begin with an audacious truth (Manifesto) that will frame our entire study on migration; then we move to address a common false belief (Myth) that impedes us from believing God's truth. We then focus on the Word of God and person of Jesus to strengthen our theological understanding of migration (Material), and conclude with practical ways in which God calls us to embody these truths in our everyday lives (Motion).

*Read the four statements and answer the reflection question. Then pause and fill out the "what if" questions in the holy imagination exercise. You'll have the opportunity to share your responses.*

| | |
|---|---|
| **MANIFESTO STATEMENT** | God wants to cultivate the heart of a migrant in each of us. |
| **MYTH STATEMENT** | "Migration is a problem." |
| **MATERIAL STATEMENT** | God honors the migrant journey and the humanity of all migrants. |
| **MOTION STATEMENT** | Migration promotes human flourishing. |

## REFLECTION

Which of these statements sticks out most to you? Why? What is your initial response to it?

# Holy Imagination Exercise

Christians throughout the ages have engaged their holy imagination, also called *faithful imagination*, to expand their capacity for understanding God and his kingdom. Because the above Manifesto, Material, and Motion statements are true (and the Myth statement is categorically false), we can be empowered to imagine how our world might be different.

*Take a few minutes to write out at least three "what if" statements that could be true if we recognized migration as part of God's story for humanity and the importance of cultivating the heart of a migrant. (Examples: What if our societies celebrated and honored migrants and immigrants? What if we learned to live with the faith, courage, and hope that so many migrants have?)*

**What if** ?

**What if** ?

**What if** ?

**What if** ?

*Share your statements with the group, as well as any thoughts or reflections this exercise prompted.*

# BENEDICTION

We have all heard many narrations, interpretations, and perspectives about migration. Approaching this subject with a fresh sense of curiosity and openness can be challenging. The good news is that our God is delighted to bestow wisdom and understanding upon us; we need only ask.

*Read this prayer of St. Augustine to close your time this week.*

***Look upon us, O Lord,***
***and let all the darkness of our souls***
***vanish before the beams of thy brightness.***
***Fill us with holy love,***
***and open to us the treasures of thy wisdom.***
***All our desire is known unto thee,***
***therefore perfect what thou hast begun,***
***and what thy Spirit has awakened us to ask in prayer.***
***We seek thy face,***
***turn thy face unto us and show us thy glory.***
***Then shall our longing be satisfied,***
***and our peace shall be perfect.***
***Amen.***

# APPLICATION ACTIVITY

## Scripture Reading and Reflection

*Set aside fifteen minutes to read and reflect on Ruth 1. Journal about the emotions Naomi and Ruth may have experienced as they moved from one place to another while experiencing loss and new relationships. We will spend more time with this passage in the next session.*

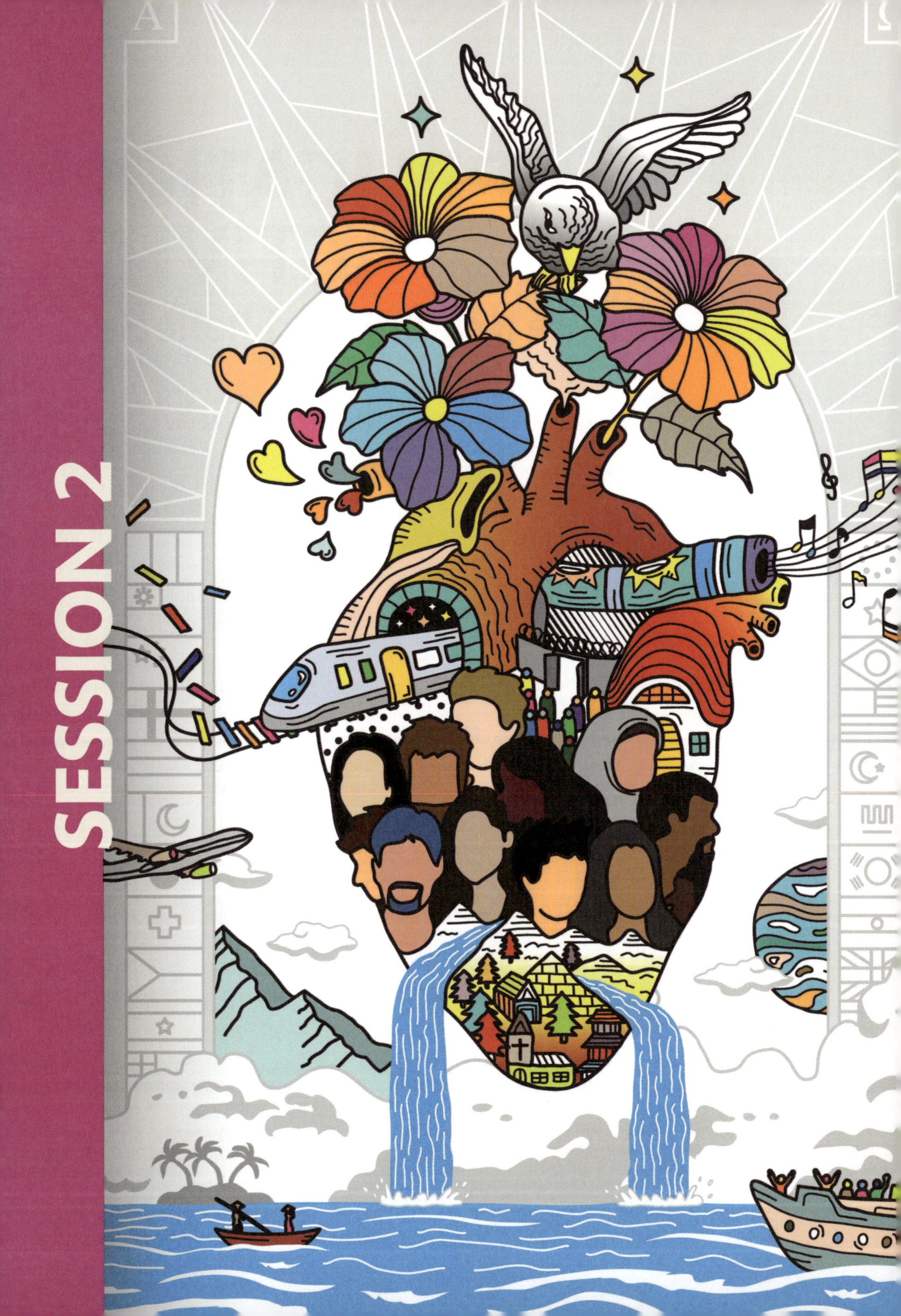

# SESSION 2

# Manifesto

## DECLARATION OF PEACE

Last week, we began to examine the central role of migration in human history as well as God's story. This session is all about the Manifesto path point, or the big idea we want to focus on. We will spend time with Scripture and an essay, both of which explore how God transforms us through migration.

# INTRODUCTION

Most of us are drawn to a sense of home. But, sometimes, moving is necessary. No matter our reasons for leaving, it is a significant and emotional transition.

God is no stranger to these feelings. In Scripture, we rarely see people staying put. Abraham, Joseph and his brothers, Naomi, Ruth, the disciples, and Paul all left familiar settings for new horizons at various points in their lives (Genesis 12:1-9; 37:12-28; 46:1-7; Ruth 1; Matthew 4:18-22; Acts 8:1-8; 13).

Migration has always been part of the human story, and it is central to the ultimate Story. Jesus was born away from his parents' home (Luke 2:1-7); fled as a young boy to another region (Matthew 2:13-15); lived his adult life constantly on the move (Matthew 8:18-20); and told his disciples to spread the good news to the ends of the earth (Acts 1:6-9). He had a particular ethnicity, homeland, and language, yet he didn't solely experience life within those boundaries. Jesus had the heart of a migrant.

Do we have this same heart? Would we allow God to cultivate the heart of a migrant in us? Jesus shows us that our belonging comes in following wherever God leads, seeking our sense of home wherever we end up.

# MANIFESTO STATEMENT

In the last session, we introduced the Manifesto statement, which provides the framework for today's Bible passage and essay. The Manifesto statement is a foundational truth that connects the dots between God, us, and migration.

*Read this statement and then pray a brief prayer to open your heart to what the Holy Spirit may want to teach you today.*

**God wants to cultivate the heart of a migrant in each of us.**

MADE FOR PAX

# SCRIPTURE READING
## Ruth 1:1-11, 14, 16-19

The book of Ruth is notable as one of the few woman-centered books of the Bible, and also for its focus on migration and interracial marriage. The book also previews the ascension of King David to the throne generations later and foreshadows the multiethnic, multicultural background of Jesus. The first chapter of Ruth provides the backstory of Naomi, her daughter-in-law Ruth, and their deep bond—all of which are critical for laying the foundation for the royal lineage of Israel.

***Read the passage below and then consider the reflection questions. As you read, circle or underline any words or phrases connected to migration and its impact on people.***

*In the days when the judges ruled, there was a famine in the land, and a certain man of Bethlehem in Judah went to live in the country of Moab, he and his wife and two sons. The name of the man was Elimelech and the name of his wife Naomi, and the names of his two sons were Mahlon and Chilion; they were Ephrathites from Bethlehem in Judah. They went into the country of Moab and remained there.*

*But Elimelech, the husband of Naomi, died, and she was left with her two sons. These took Moabite wives; the name of the one was Orpah and the name of the other Ruth. When they had lived there about ten years, both Mahlon and Chilion also died, so that the woman was left without her two sons and her husband.*

*Then she started to return with her daughters-in-law from the country of Moab, for she had heard in the country of Moab that the LORD had considered his people and given them food. So she set out from the place where she had been living, she and her two daughters-in-law, and they went on their way to go back to the land of Judah.*

*But Naomi said to her two daughters-in-law, "Go back each of you to your mother's house. May the LORD deal kindly with you, as you have dealt with the dead and with me. The LORD grant that you may find security, each of you in the house of your husband."*

*Then she kissed them, and they wept aloud. They said to her, "No, we will return with you to your people."*

*But Naomi said, "Turn back, my daughters. Why will you go with me? Do I still have sons in my womb that they may become your husbands?" . . .*

*Then they wept aloud again. Orpah kissed her mother-in-law goodbye, but Ruth clung to her. . . .*

*But Ruth said, "Do not press me to leave you, to turn back from following you! Where you go, I will go; where you lodge, I will lodge; your people shall be my people and your God my God. Where you die, I will die, and there will I be buried. May the LORD do thus to me, and more as well, if even death parts me from you!"*

*When Naomi saw that she was determined to go with her, she said no more to her. So the two of them went on until they came to Bethlehem. When they came to Bethlehem, the whole town was stirred because of them, and the women said, "Is this Naomi?"*

## REFLECTION

1. What circumstances prompted Naomi and her family to migrate to Moab and then Naomi to later return to the land of Judah?

2. Why is Ruth's decision to go with Naomi so significant? What will leaving her homeland and living in Judah require of Ruth?

# ESSAY EXCERPT

Migration today may look different from Bible times, and it often leads to particular political debates. But theologian Jules Martínez-Olivieri explains that although migration has historically been an extremely fluid concept, affected by changing borders, changing laws, and changing push-pull factors, migration has always been central to the human experience. And God shows a special love for his people when they are on the move.

***Take a few minutes to read this essay excerpt. Then we'll discuss the reflection questions that follow.***

## "Immigrants as the Face and History of Globalization"

BY JULES MARTÍNEZ-OLIVIERI

"Humanity is fundamentally a story of migration."[1]

These are the words of Moroccan American novelist and essayist Laila Lalami. Migration is an essential element of the life of peoples and a reality that shapes human history and redemptive history.

People migrate for different reasons. Sometimes they have a choice about moving; other times they are forced to move. With voluntary migration, people have reasons to either *leave* a place (push factors) or reasons to be *attracted* to a place (pull factors). Humans have been moving in response to these push and pull factors for millennia.

There are many types of borders beyond geopolitical boundaries: ideological, cultural, political, ethnic, spiritual, economic, etc. Thus, our main criterion for identifying the migrant border crosser cannot be reduced to those who simply lack residency or legal documentation in a territorially bounded sovereign country. Rather, we need to see that migration, in many forms, has always been a human reality.

## The Fact and Fluidity of Borders

Nevertheless, the concept of borders is a perpetual sociopolitical fact with an awful history of abuse and suffering designed to protect the welfare of geographically, racially, or ethnically defined nation-states. The Chinese Exclusion Act of 1882 was the first time in the United States that a "federal law proscribed [prohibited] entry of an ethnic working group on the premise that it endangered the good order of certain localities."[2] This law not only placed requirements on Chinese people trying to immigrate to the United States but also placed new requirements on Chinese who had already arrived. As economic competition and struggle increased, anti-Chinese animosity became the scapegoat for moneymaking and political gains.

Geopolitical boundaries also change over time. The US-Mexican border was not always where it is today. In 1821, the year Mexico declared its independence from Spain, its territory included California, Texas, and the land in between. However, after the Mexican-American War in 1848, 55 percent of Mexico's territory was ceded to the United States. Mexico had ended slavery by 1830; nevertheless, when White Americans formed the independent Republic of Texas, they reinstated slavery. "By the time the US annexed the territory," journalist Becky Little explains, "its enslaved population had grown from 5,000 to 30,000."[3]

Being an immigrant is not an objective status; it's a fluid designation that changes when territories change.

## PAUSE & REFLECT

**What are other examples from history or today where borders/fences/walls were used to harm a person or people group?**

## Migration Necessitates Change—for All of Us

Currently, there are more than 272 million international migrants in the world. Migration plays a major role in the economy, politics, and social structure of the majority of countries in the world. This also involves the convergences of cultures, traditions, aesthetics, art, music, values, food, and human needs. ***The increased interconnectivity caused by migration facilitates the need for—and catalyzes—the innovation of ideas, culture, and technology***.

US immigration policy, which has not been significantly updated in thirty-five years, is an area in which innovation is sorely needed. Over 10 million undocumented immigrants reside in the United States right now. Authorized immigration to the United States is generally limited to three different routes: (1) employment (where, in most cases, an employer must petition for the worker), (2) family reunification, or (3) humanitarian protection. Unfortunately, many aspiring residents are not eligible for these options, despite the fact that most immigrants to the United States have left their homeland, family, and friends due to severe economic hardship, violence, and dangerous political instability. In past times, migration was a natural respite for such conditions.

> *Migration, in many forms, has always been a human reality.*

### What Migration Means for Christians

As Christians, we cannot reduce immigrants to geopolitical conceptions. We commit atrocities and dehumanize those who are our neighbors when we see migrant foreigners as a threat, a risk, or an unknown to our "sacred" political, economic, geographical, and cultural realities and traditions.

A more humane and theological approach centers the plight of those who suffer a forced disconnection from their family, the deprived who transit to another land, and those who come seeking relationships that enhance their capacity to flourish.

***Through migration, our values, faith, and churches are renewed***. The reality of the migrant experience challenges us as Christians to be more just and charitable. We come to realize that, as the Jesuit priest Jon Sobrino beautifully states in his book *The Principle of Mercy*, "In the beginning was mercy." This mercy for the foreigner compels us to embody Jesus, announce the kingdom of God, and denounce everything that harms the vulnerable as anti-kingdom. This is achieved only when the suffering of others is internalized and becomes a joyful *orthopathos*, a passioned identification with the other for whom God's love is extended through us. Through migration, God changes our hearts.

# REFLECTION

1. What historical and theological points are missing from our current sociopolitical debates about migration? What are the consequences of most people not recognizing this broader context?

2. Jules Martínez-Olivieri says that migration necessitates change for all of us, whether we ourselves are migrants or not. How does this truth connect to God's desire for each of us to have the heart of a migrant?

# MANIFESTO STATEMENT
## REVISITED

As we prepare to close our time, we return to the foundational truth that will guide this study. Please read the Manifesto statement one more time.

**God wants to cultivate the heart of a migrant in each of us.**

*Based on what we have studied today, what does it mean to have the heart of a migrant? Share one word or phrase that, to you, encapsulates "the heart of a migrant."*

# BENEDICTION

Throughout history, recitations of shared beliefs have helped reinforce our connection to one another, no matter where we are from.

*To close this session, read this benediction.*

***Lord, help us to honor and more deeply understand our own migration stories. Help us to celebrate the mosaic of cultures, lands, and experiences that make us each unique. Foster in us the heart of a migrant: full of faith, courage, and hope in your good plans for us. Help us to find ultimate belonging in you and the family of God.***

***In the words of the author of Hebrews, we pray for the heritage of our faithful ancestors:***

***"They confessed that they were strangers and foreigners on the earth, for people who speak in this way make it clear that they are seeking a homeland. If they had been thinking of the land that they had left behind, they would have had opportunity to return. But as it is, they desire a better homeland, that is, a heavenly one. Therefore God is not ashamed to be called their God; indeed, he has***

# APPLICATION ACTIVITY

## Poetry, Art, and Reflection

*Before next week's session, listen to the poem "Welcome to my Vida!" by Frank Espinoza and take a look at the artwork by Urias Abraham. Spend a few minutes journaling about the generational effects of migration in your own family and community. Thank God for your family's migration story and ask God to cultivate the heart of a migrant in you.*

ARTWORK BY URIAS ABRAHAM

# SESSION 3

# Myth

## DISTORTION OF PEACE

In the last session, we explored the Manifesto statement: "God wants to cultivate the heart of a migrant in each of us." We studied the story of Naomi and Ruth and explored how migration has always been interwoven with human existence.

This week, we'll explore the false beliefs and counter-narratives that claim migration in and of itself is problematic. Deconstructing myths can sometimes be uncomfortable, as doing so may challenge our perspectives or what we've been taught. That's okay. We encourage you to lean into the discomfort as you reflect, ask questions, and engage with God. Pay attention to the small nudges of the Spirit through today's Scripture, essay, poem, and discussion times.

# INTRODUCTION

"They should go back to where they came from!"

This hateful sentiment has been around as long as the nation of the United States, even though most everyone in the United States, except for Native Americans, came from somewhere else.

Needless to say, this statement is far from God's heart. This rhetoric assumes migration is a problem and that we "own" the land in ways we actually don't. Our story as believers begins with God's instruction for Abram to leave the land of his ancestors and migrate to a place he had never seen (Genesis 12:1-3). God makes promises to Abram about his family, his legacy, and his relationship to the Lord; all of them began with this move.

His journey is just the first step in a long history of God's people migrating from place to place—into Egypt, the wilderness, the Promised Land, and even Babylon—and being called to care for other migrants who joined them or lived beside them along the way. Migration isn't a problem in biblical history, but a divine mandate and an integral component of walking with God.

# MYTH STATEMENT

The Myth statement is a misconception, false teaching, or lie that we frequently hear about migration. Oftentimes myths sound reasonable. But when we dig deeper, we find that they are rooted in fear, self-preservation, or misinformation. It's important for us to acknowledge and deconstruct common myths in order to create space for the truth of God to break through.

*Read the following Myth statement. Keep this statement in mind throughout this session.*

## "Migration is a problem."

# NO OTHER WAY BUT THROUGH

SEND THEM BACK

NO ILLEGAL ALIENS

THIS IS NOT YOUR HOME

WE SPEAK ENGLISH HERE

BUILD A WALL

I am going to speak very slowly as if you don't understand what I am saying

WE ONLY WANT THE GOOD ONES

Go back to your COUNTRY

WE DON'T WANT YOU HERE

*Resilient Migrant*

BY JOSUÉ CARBALLO-HUERTAS

# SCRIPTURE READING
## Genesis 12:1-10

The twelfth chapter of Genesis reflects an important turning point in the Bible. The narratives in the preceding chapters are global, cosmic stories about creation, the fall, and the expansion of humanity. But here Scripture narrows its focus to one family and their relationship with God, which sets the stage for all that is to follow.

***Read the passage below and then we'll discuss the reflection questions.***

*Now the LORD said to Abram, "Go from your country and your kindred and your father's house to the land that I will show you. I will make of you a great nation, and I will bless you and make your name great, so that you will be a blessing. I will bless those who bless you, and the one who curses you I will curse, and in you all the families of the earth shall be blessed."*

*So Abram went, as the LORD had told him, and Lot went with him. Abram was seventy-five years old when he departed from Haran. Abram took his wife Sarai and his brother's son Lot and all the possessions that they had gathered and the persons whom they had acquired in Haran, and they set forth to go to the land of Canaan.*

*When they had come to the land of Canaan, Abram passed through the land to the place at Shechem, to the oak of Moreh. At that time the Canaanites were in the land. Then the LORD appeared to Abram and said, "To your offspring I will give this land."*

*So he built there an altar to the LORD, who had appeared to him. From there he moved on to the hill country on the east of Bethel and pitched his tent, with Bethel on the west and Ai on the east, and there he built an altar to the LORD and invoked the name of the LORD. And Abram journeyed on by stages toward the Negeb.*

*Now there was a famine in the land. So Abram went down to Egypt to reside there as an alien, for the famine was severe in the land.*

## REFLECTION

1. Historians estimate that Abram lived more than four thousand years ago. What do you think it would have been like for Abram to migrate to a new land?

2. Why do you think God called Abram to a new place in order to establish a new people? How do you see this call affecting the major events of the rest of Scripture?

# ESSAY EXCERPT

In the United States, passionate, emotional debates about immigration are commonplace. But what are the fears, anxieties, and beliefs driving these strong opinions? In this essay, Pastor Gabriel Salguero breaks down the key myths that lead Americans to oppose immigration reform or immigration of any kind.

***Spend a few minutes reading this excerpt. As you read, circle or underline any sentences or phrases that you find particularly meaningful.***

## "Immigration Reform: Beyond Myths and Fears"

BY GABRIEL SALGUERO

Though a majority of Americans favor immigration reform, it has become a third rail in our national conversation. This is one of the most divisive issues in contemporary American political life. And when it comes to solving this intractable challenge with bipartisan legislation, there has been much heat and little light.

### A Call for Moral Courage

Our nation is in profound need of truth-telling and spiritual and moral courage that charts a way forward beyond the present stagnating fear. Elected officials need to be willing to tell the truth about the ruinous impacts of our current immigration policies on immigrants and our nation. They must seriously deal with the harmful root causes of displacement around the world through substantive foreign policy. And this must be coupled with the courage to legislate rather than engage in partisan hyperbolic rhetoric.

One of the major hurdles is fear. ***Fear obfuscates our ability to see and speak with each other.***

The antidote is courage—courage to tell the truth about the state of our immigration system and to distinguish between arguments based on facts and those based on myths. Every citizen can help listen and highlight the stories of our immigrant neighbors, coworkers, and family members. For genuine change, we need a grassroots groundswell of pastors, churches, business owners, teachers, parents, and all people of goodwill to say our nation can and must do better.

Christian public speech on immigration has too frequently come before understanding, and the damage has been considerable. Before we speak, we must seek to know and understand.

## PAUSE & REFLECT

**How have you seen fear of immigration expressed? What harm has it done?**

Here are three of the most harmful myths that continue to create obstacles to more just and humane immigration policies in America and the truths necessary to counter these nefarious narratives.

### 1. The National Identity Myth

Certain segments of our society fear the loss of an idealized or romanticized national identity. With the exception of indigenous peoples and enslaved African peoples, the United States is a nation of immigrants. Any idealized depiction of a homogeneous nation is ahistorical. Any initiatives toward bipartisan immigration reform must squarely address the myth of a culturally and racially homogenous nation.

In response to anxieties about national cohesion, we need a clear vision that our national unity—*E pluribus unum*, or "out of many, one"—is not based on culture or race but a shared commitment to a diverse democratic society. Diversity enriches our democracy and reflects the Christian ethic of unity across diversity evidenced in the kingdom of God in Revelation 7:9 (NIV), which says "from every nation, tribe, people and language."

*Love thy neighbor does not end at our borders.*

## 2. The Economic Myth

Immigrants, many believe, are a burden to our economic system.

However, studies show that the millions of immigrants already in the United States are a net positive to the American economy. According to bipartisan political organization FWD.us, "Immigrants added $2 trillion to the US GDP in 2016 and $458.7 billion in state, local, and federal taxes in 2018." In addition, immigrants are vital to creating jobs across our country. The bipartisan research firm New American Economy reports that, in 2017, 8 million people were employed at immigrant-owned businesses, which earned $1.3 trillion in revenue.

A new immigration system that integrates immigrants will continue to add hundreds of millions of dollars to the economy. We can and should have the creative genius to make this a win-win for all.

As a Jesus-follower, I believe economics is not the moral arbiter of national decisions. ***Christianity demands hospitality, and hospitality requires sacrifice.***

## 3. The Law-and-Order Myth

Some fear that if we reward undocumented immigrants with a path to citizenship or a restitution-based integration policy, the nation will set a dangerous precedent. Perhaps the resulting flow of immigration will overwhelm us.

We cannot ignore the fact that broken laws hurt people. Theologian Saint Augustine reminds us that "an unjust law is no law at all." The book of Romans tells us to submit to authority (Romans 13) but at the same time reminds us not to conform to patterns that are incongruent with our gospel values (Romans 12).

Historically, our nation has periodically modernized its immigration systems in response to economic demands and global migration flows. Immigration reform can include requiring back-tax payments, penalties for employers who have circumvented the system, and humane border supervision.

Reform must include respect for the rule of law and humane integration of immigrants. We should continuously ask: What laws should we pass that treat our immigrant neighbors with dignity and respect, while dealing with the root causes that displace millions of God's children around the world?

## REFLECTION

1. Why do you think fears and anxieties about immigration persist in the United States?

2. Salguero says that "the antidote is courage." What are tangible ways in which we can nurture this courage within ourselves, our community members, and our leaders?

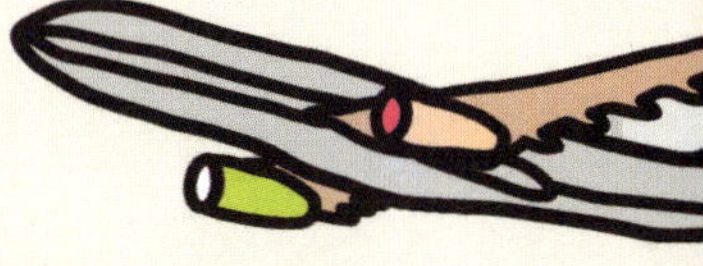

# POETRY

Poet Jean Nangwala, who is originally from Zambia, takes on the questions and comments often directed toward her since she immigrated to the United States.

*Listen to Nangwala's recording of the poem. Then we'll discuss the questions below.*

## REFLECTION

1. What is the cost—for individual migrants and for receiving cultures—when we are not hospitable toward immigrants?

2. Based on what we've covered in this session, what are the true "problems" related to migration? What could it look like to address those problems?

# BENEDICTION

Entering the debate about immigration—which often elicits anger, frustration, and fear—can be daunting. As Jesus-followers, we need Christ to influence our understanding of migration and also our posture of engagement with those around us, no matter where they stand on the issue. We need grace, patience, and perseverance—and a good dose of courage.

*Read this prayer, adapted from the Book of Common Prayer, as you conclude this session.*

***Go forth into the world in peace.***
***Be of good courage.***
***Hold fast that which is good.***
***Render to no one evil for evil.***
***Strengthen the fainthearted.***
***Support the weak.***
***Help the afflicted.***
***Show love to everyone.***
***Love and serve the Lord,***
***rejoicing in the power of the Holy Spirit;***
***and the blessing of almighty God,***
***the Father, the Son, and the Holy Spirit,***
***be among you and remain with you always.***
***Amen.***

# APPLICATION ACTIVITY

## Case Study & Lament

ARTWORK BY MONDO SCOTT

When rulers and governments act to encourage or curtail migration, the effects reverberate across societies and generations. As people of God, we are encouraged to express solidarity with the vulnerable and hurting through the ancient biblical practice of lament.

***Spend a few minutes reading this case study of the 1882 Chinese Exclusion Act by Dorcas Cheng-Tozun while also viewing the accompanying images by Mondo Scott. Then, write or verbally express lament for the harm caused by this law and other immigration laws like it. You can use the format below, which is based on laments in Psalms, or you can write your own prayer of lament.***

1. Opening Address: What role does God play in this situation? What title is appropriate as an appeal to God's character?
2. Complaint: Authentically communicate the source of your sorrow, grief, and anger.
3. Confession of Trust: Express your desire to trust; remember how God has been faithful in the past.
4. Petition for Help: How do you want God to act? Where do you want to see change?
5. Vow of Praise: Look beyond the current circumstances and acknowledge how God is worthy of praise.

NO!
Streets at 7:30
express your
question.
NO!

An American Injustice
The Chinese Exclusion Act
~ Lasting Legacy ~
I AM AN AMERICAN

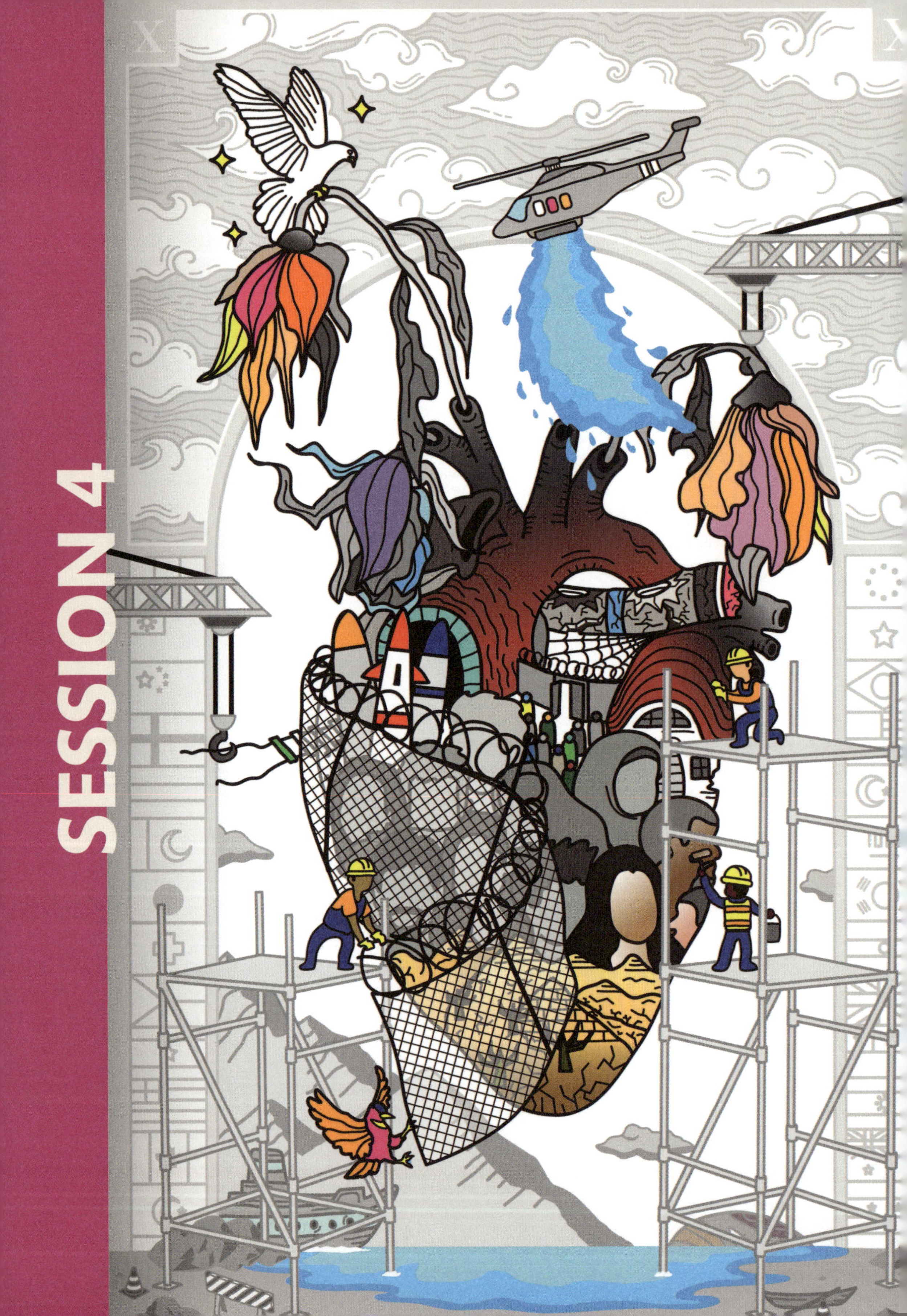
SESSION 4

# Material

## EXPRESSIONS OF PEACE

So far we've looked at Manifesto and Myth, exploring a central truth about migration and deconstructing a persistent false belief about migration. We've seen how migration was central to the formation of God's people and the lineage of Jesus. We examined the fears and concerns that drive opposition to migration and began to explore humane, God-honoring immigration policies.

This week we move to the Material path point of our discipleship pathway. We will take a closer look at what Scripture says explicitly about migrants and migration, and how we as followers of Jesus should respond.

# INTRODUCTION

In the Old Testament, Yahweh frequently taught the Israelites to "love the stranger, for you were strangers in the land of Egypt" (Deuteronomy 10:19; see also Exodus 22:21; Leviticus 19:34).

God knows that humans have a tendency to accept our own humanity while forgetting the humanity of people who don't look like us. God continually reminded the ancient Israelites to treat others as they would want to be treated. After all, their people had a long history as migrants, exiles, and refugees (Deuteronomy 5:15; 16:12; Psalm 137:1).

Whether we have traveled far from home or we have heard the stories of our parents, grandparents, or great-grandparents, we are called to remember stories of migration and honor the journeys of others (Deuteronomy 6:20-23; 26:4-11; Jeremiah 51:50). We are instructed to treat one another how we would want to be treated if we were in a new land (Leviticus 19:34; Matthew 25:35; Hebrews 13:2).

God honors our journeys. He is with us, and at work in us, every step of the way.

# MATERIAL STATEMENT

The Material path point focuses on biblically based truths about migration. It provides a foundation for us to value the migration experiences in our own families and our broader communities.

*Read the Material Statement. Keep this statement in mind throughout this session.*

**God honors the migrant journey and the humanity of all migrants.**

# SCRIPTURE READING

## Deuteronomy 10:12-13, 17-22

The book of Deuteronomy consists of Moses' last instructions to the Hebrew people before they enter the Promised Land. Biblical scholars consider it a record of the covenant between God and his people, laying out how they should live as representatives of God on earth.

***Read the passage below and then we'll discuss the reflection questions.***

*So now, O Israel, what does the LORD your God require of you? Only to fear the LORD your God, to walk in all his ways, to love him, to serve the LORD your God with all your heart and with all your soul, and to keep the commandments of the LORD your God and his decrees that I am commanding you today, for your own well-being. . . .*

*For the LORD your God is God of gods and Lord of lords, the great God, mighty and awesome, who is not partial and takes no bribe, who executes justice for the orphan and the widow, and who loves the strangers, providing them food and clothing. You shall also love the stranger, for you were strangers in the land of Egypt. You shall fear the LORD your God; him you shall serve; to him you shall hold fast; and by his name you shall swear. He is your praise; he is your God who has done for you these great and awesome things that your own eyes have seen. Your ancestors went down to Egypt seventy persons, and now the LORD your God has made you as numerous as the stars in heaven.*

## REFLECTION

1. What reasons does this passage give for loving the stranger? Why do you think this is so important to God?

2. What do these commands tell us about the character of God and his view of migrants, refugees, and exiles?

# ESSAY EXCERPT

When read through the lens of migration, the narratives of Scripture can take on new meaning. The biblical characters seem more vulnerable and courageous; the places aren't abstractions but homelands or new regions. In this essay excerpt, immigration activist Paola Fuentes Gleghorn walks through some of the most well-known stories in the Old and New Testaments, connecting migration with divine grace, from ancient times to today.

***Take a few minutes to read Gleghorn's piece. As you read, underline or circle any words or phrases that stick out to you. Then we'll come back together as a group to discuss the reflection questions.***

## "The Bible: Stories about Immigrant People by Immigrant People"

BY PAOLA FUENTES GLEGHORN

Migration is not a new or modern phenomenon. Throughout human history, people have migrated from one place to another. In harmony with creation and the native people of the land, all people have the right to migrate, whether for survival or flourishing.

### Migration as Grace

The Bible is full of stories about immigrants and by immigrants. The message is clear: migration is central to our faith. God cares and provides for migrant people, calls us to welcome and support immigrants, and uses our stories of migration to further his reconciling work.

Dr. Robert Chao Romero speaks of migration as grace and explains that God uses the migration process to extend his unmerited favor, love, and compassion to both immigrants and their host countries.[1] We see this clearly in the story of Abraham and Sarah in the Old Testament. God calls Abraham to migrate from his country and from his people and household to an unknown destination that God will show him. God also tells him, "I will make of you a great nation, and I will bless you, and make your name great, so that you will be a blessing . . . and in you all the families of the earth shall be blessed" (Genesis 12:1-3). God's grace and blessings come hand in hand for the immigrants, but also for those in their host country.

## PAUSE & REFLECT

How have you or your family been blessed by immigrants in your community?

## Migration as Blessing

**Blessing is woven into the story of migration.**

Blessing is woven into the story of migration. When God commanded Israel to treat immigrant people the same as native Israelites, there was a provision for a blessed community. In both Exodus 12:49 and Leviticus 24:22, God tells Israel that "there shall be one law for the native-born and for the alien who resides among you." Additionally, the people of Israel had to make sure that immigrants, orphans, and widows had a way to provide for themselves. The law required Israel to provide for immigrant people in the same way they provided for the Levites, their priests.

***These commands flow from a consistent theme in the Bible: everyone should be treated with dignity and equity.*** He names particular groups explicitly so we can't forget about them. And orphans, widows, and immigrant people share something in common. They are separated from their families, either by distance or death, which can leave them vulnerable to exploitation.

## Jesus the Migrant

Jesus himself identifies with the stories of immigrant people who are fleeing violence. Migration is a key part of Jesus' life, from conception to death and resurrection. Joseph and Mary traveled while Mary was pregnant. The three of them migrated again when Jesus was an infant to flee persecution. As an adult, Jesus traveled widely, even venturing into the enemy land of Samaria. Then he traversed the depths of hell, returned to earth, and finally ascended to heaven.

Throughout the New Testament, the authors write about hospitality. In Romans 12:9-13, we are told to "hate evil and love good, to serve the lord and rejoice in hope, and to extend hospitality to strangers." In Hebrews 13:1-3, we are told to "show hospitality to strangers, because in doing this some have entertained angels without knowing it." The Greek word for *hospitality* in Hebrews 13:1 is *philoxenia*, which means "to love the foreigner." The word *entertained*, used just afterward in Hebrews 13:3, is *xenisantes*, which means "receiving the foreigner."

Jesus' reconciliation work is not just to reconcile us to God, but also to reconcile and unite us with each other across divisions or borders.

## Migration Strengthens the Church

When we migrate to a new place or when we welcome and fully embrace immigrant people, our faith is made stronger. Through the journey, our trust in God and God's people grows. Many immigrant people talk about how their faith was a part of what kept them moving forward during the hard trip to migrate to another place.

***When we migrate or when we welcome immigrant people, our faith communities are made stronger.*** In literal ways, immigrant people are helping our churches grow. In 2013, 60 percent of all immigrant people arriving in the United States identified as Christian.

More importantly, stories of migration teach us about God's character. God is a God of creativity and unity. In order to see all aspects of who God is, we need to interact with the diversity of people and cultures that God created, treating each other with equity and finding unity across differences.

## REFLECTION

1. **Why do you think migration particularly creates opportunities for God to extend his grace to humanity?**

2. **When you examine the centrality of migration to the gospel story and the work of God, how does this change the way you read Scripture? How does it affect the way you think about migration?**

# POETRY

Through verse, poet and educator Michael Frazier reflects on his experience as a Black man living and working in Japan. Listen to his poem.

***Afterward, we'll discuss the kinds of transformation (for both individuals and communities) that are only made possible through migration, and how we see God's heart through this transformation.***

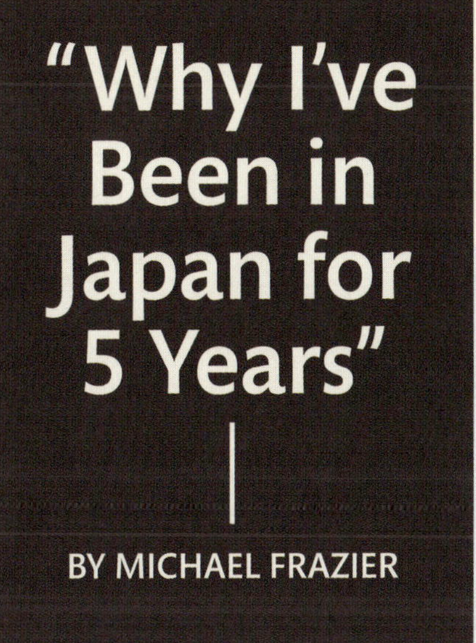

ARTWORK BY MONDO SCOTT

*Artwork*
BY URIAS ABRAHAM

# BENEDICTION

The call to love, embrace, and honor migrants and their journeys can sometimes stretch us beyond what's comfortable. We all need to lean on the love and grace that flows abundantly from God to see the imago Dei in those who come from different places, whether we ourselves are migrants or not.

*Read this short benediction to close this session.*

***Shape our hearts to receive and share.***

***Teach us to open our homes and lives.***

***Bring to our minds memories of your goodness and presence in hardship.***

***Guide us in love for our neighbors and ourselves.***

***Train us to walk in the ways of our migrant Lord.***

***Amen.***

# APPLICATION ACTIVITY

## Reading and Self-Examination

Migration is a challenging issue in large part because it affects much of what we hold dear: our communities, our identities, our wealth, and the land that we consider home. Entering into the conversation about migration requires understanding our own attachments to these things and how willing we are to prioritize God and our fellow human beings over them.

*Take some time to read this short excerpt from the essay "Land, Covenant, and Humane Policies for Migrants" by Noemi Vega Quinones. Then come before God however you feel most comfortable—through prayer, by journaling, on a walk—to reflect on the questions that follow.*

### "Land, Covenant, and Humane Policies for Migrants"

BY NOEMI VEGA QUINONES

God is the owner of the land but also miraculously chose to become God With Us as a migrant. God is aware of the vulnerability, risk, and exposure of the migrant experience. God also chooses to remain present during this experience as Immanuel with all who call on the name of Jesus. As a result, God compels Christian partnership with the sojourner and teaches us how to steward the land. Lutheran theologian Munther Isaac intricately describes God's relationship with the lands of the earth in his book *The Other Side of the Wall*. Isaac asserts that the Yawhistic treatment of the lands reflects a unique authority.

Christians, therefore, are called to remember this divine ownership and ask the Lord for wisdom on how to steward the lands with God's justice and righteousness.

For those who do not maintain this holy covenant with God, there are consequences. Ill treatment of God and God's neighbor will impact the health of the land. ***Christians are called to consider how to live on the land in our countries in a way that reflects our covenant with God and the commandment to love our neighbor as ourselves.***

## REFLECTION

1. When you think about the land where you currently reside, whose land do you think of it as? What fears, hopes, assumptions, and beliefs are at the root of this way of thinking?

2. To honor migrants as God calls us to, what sacrifices might you need to make? How might you need to rethink your sense of ownership, identity, and security?

# SESSION 5

# MOTION

## EMBODIMENT OF PEACE

In the previous four sessions, we've looked at how God wants to cultivate the heart of a migrant in each of us. We've challenged the myth that human migration is a problem with the truth that human movement is deeply interwoven into the story of God's people and the life of Jesus.

This session focuses on the Motion path point and how we can respond to what we've learned. We will look at the mutual flourishing that immigration advances and ways to support migration that promote opportunities for people to connect with and receive from God. No matter your own family's immigration story, God calls us to honor and stand in solidarity with the migrants in our communities.

# INTRODUCTION

Jesus could have come into this world any number of ways, but he chose to be a migrant. He underwent spiritual migration—leaving behind close communion with the Father and becoming a mere man (John 3:13). He also experienced physical migration throughout his earthly life: to Bethlehem, to Egypt, and even to Jerusalem to celebrate feasts as often as three times a year (Luke 2:41-52; John 2:13-25; 7:9-14).

During his ministry, Jesus was constantly on the road (Matthew 8:20).

None of this was by mistake or happenstance. Hundreds of years before Jesus walked those dusty roads in Roman Palestine, the prophets declared that he would wander for the sake of the world he created (Isaiah 9:1; Hosea 11:1). If Jesus came to show us how to live, then his example points to how migration promotes the flourishing God has planned for all of us.

# MOTION STATEMENT

The final statement in our discipleship pathway, the Motion statement, invites us to embody the truths we have studied.

*Read the following statement. Keep this statement in mind during today's session.*

## Migration promotes human flourishing.

MADE FOR PAX

# SCRIPTURE READING
## Matthew 4:12-25

As recorded in the Gospel of Matthew, Jesus begins his ministry being baptized by his cousin John, then fasting and being tempted by the devil in the wilderness for forty days. He returns and learns that John has been arrested. With the words "Repent, for the kingdom of heaven has come near," Jesus continues John's work but also pursues ministry in his own way.

***Read the passage below. As you read, circle or underline any references to Jesus or others traveling and migrating. Then we'll discuss the reflection questions.***

*Now when Jesus heard that John had been arrested, he withdrew to Galilee. He left Nazareth and made his home in Capernaum by the sea, in the territory of Zebulun and Naphtali, so that what had been spoken through the prophet Isaiah might be fulfilled:*

*"Land of Zebulun, land of Naphtali, on the road by the sea, across the Jordan, Galilee of the gentiles—the people who sat in darkness have seen a great light, and for those who sat in the region and shadow of death light has dawned."*

*From that time Jesus began to proclaim, "Repent, for the kingdom of heaven has come near." As he walked by the Sea of Galilee, he saw two brothers, Simon, who is called Peter, and Andrew his brother, casting a net into the sea—for they were fishers. And he said to them, "Follow me, and I will make you fishers of people." Immediately they left their nets and followed him. As he went from there, he saw two other brothers, James son of Zebedee and his brother John, in the boat with their father Zebedee, mending their nets, and he called them. Immediately they left the boat and their father and followed him.*

*Jesus went throughout all Galilee, teaching in their synagogues and proclaiming the good news of the kingdom and curing every disease and every sickness among the people. So his fame spread throughout all Syria, and they brought to him all the sick, those who were afflicted with various diseases and pains, people possessed by demons or having epilepsy or afflicted with paralysis, and he cured them. And great crowds followed him from Galilee, the Decapolis, Jerusalem, Judea, and from beyond the Jordan.*

## REFLECTION

1. Ancient historian Josephus tells us that, during this time, the region of Galilee had about three million residents, mostly Gentiles but with many Jews among them, spread across more than two hundred large villages. It was ruled by the ironfisted Herod, who had imprisoned John. Nazareth was Jesus' hometown; Capernaum was a large village in Galilee (but far smaller than Jerusalem). What is the significance of Jesus' move from Nazareth to Capernaum? What risks is he taking?

2. How are leaving home, traveling, and migrating integral to Jesus' broader ministry? How does his willingness to move benefit others?

# ESSAY EXCERPT

In this essay, writer and immigration advocate Gena Ruocco Thomas describes how our cultures and societies have been transformed by migration over time. Everything from our food and music to language and technologies have benefitted from traditions and ideas brought from one region or country to another. And when we migrate or welcome immigrants, we ourselves are transformed.

***Read through this essay excerpt. Then we'll discuss the reflection questions.***

## "Migration as Discipleship into Christlikeness"

BY GENA RUOCCO THOMAS

Seeds carry the essence of their soil with them wherever they go. Our futures follow the trajectory our pasts set out, and our world is what it presently is because of it.

Migration plays a critical role in promoting human flourishing, as different cultures bring varying perspectives on all aspects of life, from the trivial (like how to make the best cup of coffee) to the life-changing (like how my perception of America was unknowingly exceptionalist). In my own migrations to Italy, Honduras, and Mexico, I learned to mother, cook, visit, grocery shop, welcome, worship, teach, speak, and befriend more fully.

Economic flourishing also increases because of migration.

Yet aspects of human flourishing that come from migration are often resisted. The power-holding culture can be hostile to how migration brings changes. Laila Lalami, Moroccan American novelist, writes, "Immigrants are expected, over an undefined period, to become like other Americans, a process metaphorically described as a melting pot. But what this means, in practice, remains unsettled. . . . ***It should be clear by now that assimilation is primarily about power.***"[1]

## PAUSE & REFLECT

How have you or people you know felt pressured to assimilate into majority culture?

When we look at the book of Daniel, we recognize the connection between assimilation and power right away. Daniel was immediately given an assimilated name, Belteshazzar, when he began working for the Babylonian king. Daniel had to be cunning in his approach not to assimilate, as the guard in charge of him was afraid of King Nebuchadnezzar's power (Daniel 1:10). That fear was not unmerited, as Daniel's fellow Israelites, Hananiah, Mishael, and Azariah, are later thrown into a fiery furnace for their refusal to spiritually assimilate. The Israelites here embody Christ's wisdom of learning to be as innocent as doves and as shrewd as snakes.

*Migration plays a critical role in promoting human flourishing, as different cultures bring varying perspectives on all aspects of life.*

Migration brings new opportunities—culturally, economically, and spiritually. But those come often at great cost: assimilation, family separation, loss of identity and connections to languages, lands, and people. We should acknowledge and lament the personal and cultural cost of migration. When we choose to lament together, we learn to see our migrating neighbors as whole human beings. We learn to actually love the sojourner (Deuteronomy 10:19), weep with those who weep (Romans 12:15), and help others get ahead (Philippians 2:4). When those who have never migrated learn to lament with those who have, confession follows: We confess the ways we've expected unjust assimilation. We confess the ways we've perpetuated stereotypes. We confess the ways we've benefitted from denigrating migrants. Lament and confession make room for a deeper flourishing many Christians have yet to experience.

Because of the Great Migration, when 6 million African Americans migrated from the South to the North and the West during the twentieth century, opportunities that didn't exist before were created. God-given

talent that was always there blossomed, as seen in jazz music, novels, memoirs, and art from this time. Yet flourishing was also truncated. Injustice was exposed in new ways, as certain dominant forces resisted the influx of sojourners.

***Migration has a way of pinpointing our cultural myths as they rub against other cultural narratives.*** If we are perceptive and intentional, this awareness will shed light on our cultural idols, and give us a mirror to see how much our cultural identity shapes our faith.

When we look at Acts 8, we see that the Ethiopian eunuch who had come to Jerusalem to worship (Acts 8:27) is baptized by Philip, which begins the history of the Ethiopian Orthodox Tewahedo Church. Philip, led by the Spirit, shatters previously held, culturally exclusive traditions that suggested the eunuch should not have been allowed to be baptized. Spiritual inclusion comes by way of an outsider looking in and sincerely questioning, "What would keep me from being baptized?" (Acts 8:36 CEB).

Migration shapes and molds the world as we know it; and if we allow it, it will shape, mold, and broaden our own flourishing. Whether we've migrated or not, migration disciples us into more full and aware human beings. We more closely resemble the kingdom of God not only when we welcome the changing landscape migration brings, but when we allow ourselves to be changed for the better by that landscape: to be ushered into new cultures, to see the injustice of assimilation, to step down from our cultural pedestals, to stand for the equality of all people.

## REFLECTION

1. Despite the many different forms of human flourishing (individual and collective) that result from migration, significant resistance to migration persists. What is at the root of such resistance? How does assimilation harm both immigrants and the receiving cultures?

2. If we are to be people who enable and celebrate the flourishing that can result from migration, what should our posture be? What could we practically do?

# VISIO DIVINA

Visio divina means "holy seeing." If you are familiar with lectio divina ("holy reading"), visio divina is a similar meditative process but with images instead of text. This is an opportunity to be present to your own thoughts and emotions, and to be present to what the Spirit may be saying to you.

*Spend about three minutes viewing this path point art by Jee Wook Lee. Begin by taking a few deep breaths and inviting the Spirit to speak to you. Then, let your eyes wander around the image or settle on particular parts of the image as you feel led. Listen for what the Spirit may want to say to you about migration, human flourishing, and your place in this aspect of the story of God.*

*Afterward, you'll have the opportunity to share your thoughts and reflections for a few minutes.*

ARTWORK BY JEE WOOK LEE

# BENEDICTION

The call to follow Jesus often encompasses a both/and approach rather than either-or. We are encouraged to love and be loved, to go and to stay, to celebrate and lament, to promote diversity and unity.

*As you end this session, pray this benediction from Gordon College.*

***God, lover of all people, Creator of all nations,***

***We praise you for all that you have made.***

***Thank you for the rich mosaic that is the body of Christ.***

***Thank you for difference amidst unity, for unity amidst difference.***

***Give us a spirit of understanding and appreciation of each other.***

***Help us to see your image clearly in those around us.***

***Bless us now, and may we declare your praises with our whole lives,***

***through our risen Lord Jesus.***

***Amen.***

# APPLICATION ACTIVITY

## Prayer Walk

*Set aside at least thirty minutes to spend in a vibrant neighborhood or town center near where you live.*

*Start with a brief prayer, asking God to give you divine perception to recognize how migration has promoted flourishing in your own community.*

*Slowly walk through the area and observe the ways in which immigrants and immigrant cultures have contributed to the formation of this place; consider the people, architecture, shops, restaurants, offices, trees and flowers, food, music, languages, and more.*

*As you walk, thank God for the beautiful, diverse representation of his image, creativity, and love in all that you see, hear, touch, and experience.*

# SESSION 6
# Closing

We've reached the final session in our six-week study on migration. We've covered a lot of content in the past five sessions. We've explored how migration is central to the biblical story, beginning with Abraham and through the lives of Jesus and his disciples. Migration transforms our hearts and our societies, and teaches us more about who God is and our identity in him.

In session five, we began to focus on how migration promotes human flourishing. Today we will look more closely at our role in promoting that flourishing, and how we can continue to pursue it in the coming weeks.

# INTRODUCTION

Migration is a natural—and biblical—aspect of human existence, through which God can powerfully work. Individuals, families, and communities are remade by migration, as the blending of histories and cultures enriches our knowledge and grows our empathy. In addition, the kingdom of God transforms through migration: as people bring their faith stories to new places; as church bodies welcome new brothers and sisters; as ever more aspects of God's character and image are revealed in our shared diversity.

The courageous journey of migration, with all its risks and challenges, draws us closer to God, and draws us closer to the heart of God. We are a people whose ultimate belonging is in him, and we fully embody our identity as children of God no matter where we are physically located. There is no border or geography that can separate us from the love of God—he travels with us and in us as we join humanity's story of movement and transformation.

# PATH POINT STATEMENTS
## Revisited

The path point statements have provided a framework for our learning throughout this study. Let's review the four statements as we process through what we've learned.

*Read each statement and then we'll discuss the following questions.*

| | |
|---|---|
| **MANIFESTO STATEMENT** | God wants to cultivate the heart of a migrant in each of us. |
| **MYTH STATEMENT** | "Migration is a problem." |
| **MATERIAL STATEMENT** | God honors the migrant journey and the humanity of all migrants. |
| **MOTION STATEMENT** | Migration promotes human flourishing. |

## REFLECTION

1. What are the most significant things you have learned about migration over the course of this study?

2. How have your views on different aspects of migration (immigrants, culture, causes of migration, laws, policies, theology, etc.) been impacted?

3. What additional questions do you still have around the topic of migration? How could you seek out answers to those questions?

# DISCOVERING IMMIGRANTS IN YOUR COMMUNITY

*Take about fifteen minutes to look at this tool from the Migration Policy Institute, which provides statistics on immigration by US state.*

1. Select your own state, and then select (All Counties) from the dropdown menu. This will tell you which counties in your state have the highest number of recent immigrants. Are your county or your neighboring counties on this list? Why might this be the case?
2. Next, based on your knowledge, select countries of origin that you think the immigrants in your area are from. Look at the list of counties that show up with each country of origin you examine. Are the counties in your area on these lists? How does your county compare with others in your state?
3. Take some time to discuss what you saw. Did anything surprise you? How do these statistics affect how you see your local community, your region, and your state?

# REACHING OUT TO IMMIGRANTS IN YOUR COMMUNITY

The call of hospitality for the immigrant is for all of us, and it can be answered by all of us through many acts of kindness, generosity, and service. But where to begin? Immigration advocate and pastor Kristel Acevedo shares five practical ways that we can love the immigrants among us in her guide, "From Strangers to Friends."

*On your own, spend at least ten minutes looking at and reflecting on Acevedo's description of three of these steps. Is there someone around you that you could extend care to? Are there spaces where you could be an advocate and friend? What would you consider doing, individually or as a group? Write down your ideas in the spaces provided.*

## 1. Get to know their stories.

When getting to know our immigrant neighbors, we can ask them about their unique stories without trying to fit them into a box or assimilate them into our culture. We can allow space for them to simply share as we listen.

Most likely, you have a neighbor, coworker, or fellow church member who is an immigrant. Offer to take them out for coffee. Be honest and open up about your own story. Vulnerability breeds intimacy. Ask them questions about their country of origin. Learn a few words in their language. Always maintain a tone that is kind, welcoming, and curious. This is not an interrogation; it's two new friends getting to know each other. In the space below, write the names of some people you want to connect with.

## 2. Serve them with love.

In your community, you may find lawyers who work pro bono with immigrants to help them navigate the complicated legal system. Churches may also provide Bible studies or other resources for the immigrant community.

Some have started nonprofit organizations to serve immigrants, meeting practical needs such as healthcare, food, water, education, translation services, and more. If you have skills, goods, or services to contribute, partnering with an organization could help maximize your impact.

Think of ways God is calling you to step in the gap for immigrants. It can be as simple as offering a ride to work, buying groceries for the week, or helping them register kids for school. Perhaps you can even ask your immigrant friends directly how you can best serve them. In the space below, identify the service opportunities that you want to explore.

## 3. Invite them to the table.

Our immigrant neighbors have a lot to offer us. They have wonderful insights to share and can lead at an incredible capacity.

Look for the specific way God shines through the immigrants around you. Create space for them and invite them to sit at the head of the table. Doing so makes us all better. We can have immigrants on our church boards, invite them to speak at conferences, and join community groups. We can intentionally recruit immigrants to join organizations we serve so they can share their unique perspective and wealth of knowledge. In the space below, identify ways you can amplify and learn from immigrants.

# COMMITMENTS

*Spend a few minutes sharing how this exercise was for you. How did you feel as you did this? What most excites you? Most concerns you?*

*Share at least one way in which you want to extend love and hospitality to immigrants in your community. How do you want to support one another in these commitments? Is there anything you could consider doing together as a group? Write your commitments below.*

# CLOSING PRAYER

*Spend a few minutes in prayer thanking God for his great love and care for immigrants, and the flourishing he desires all of us to experience as a result of migration.*

*Begin and end your prayer time with these words from Deuteronomy 10:17-19:*

***For the LORD your God is God of gods and Lord of lords, the great God, mighty and awesome, who is not partial and takes no bribe, who executes justice for the orphan and the widow, and who loves the strangers, providing them food and clothing. You shall also love the stranger, for you were strangers in the land of Egypt.***

# BENEDICTION

*As you close your time and finish this study, you can listen to Jean Nangwala's recitation of "**The Immigrants' Creed**."*[1]

*I believe in Almighty God,*
*who guided the people in exile and in exodus,*
*the God of Joseph in Egypt and Daniel in Babylon,*
*the God of foreigners and immigrants.*
*I believe in Jesus Christ,*
*a displaced Galilean,*
*who was born away from his people and his home,*
*who fled his country with his parents when his life was in danger,*
*and returning to his own country suffered the oppression*
*of the tyrant Pontius Pilate, the servant of a foreign power,*
*who then was persecuted, beaten, and finally tortured,*
*accused and condemned to death unjustly.*
*But on the third day, this scorned Jesus rose from the dead,*
*not as a foreigner but to offer us citizenship in heaven.*
*I believe in the Holy Spirit,*
*the eternal immigrant from God's kingdom among us,*
*who speaks all languages, lives in all countries,*
*and reunites all races.*
*I believe that the church is the secure home*
*for the foreigner and for all believers who constitute it,*
*who speak the same language and have the same purpose.*
*I believe that the communion of the saints begins*
*when we accept the diversity of the saints.*
*I believe in the forgiveness of sin, which makes us all equal,*
*and in reconciliation, which identifies us more*
*than does race, language, or nationality.*
*I believe that in the resurrection*
*God will unite us as one people*
*in which all are distinct*
*and all are alike at the same time.*
*Beyond this world, I believe in life eternal*
*in which no one will be an immigrant*
*but all will be citizens of God's kingdom,*
*which will never end. Amen.*

# ADDITIONAL RESOURCES

"Migration Stories from Around the World," audio narratives by Christina Lee, Jai Patel, Karla Mendoza, Martha Gatkuoch, and Vivian Gee

"The Most Restrictive Border in the World," a video interview with Helen Lee

"On the Front Lines: Grief and Transformation in Serving Immigrants," a video panel with Blanca Castillo, Guillermo Torres, and Jonathan Fung

"Every Flower Starts as a Seed that Chooses to Stay Still & Wait," a poem by Michael Frazier

"In Their Own Words: Cross-Cultural Collaboration and Friendship for the Kingdom," audio dialogues by Hogan Bassey, Matt Elsberry, Marcos Canales, and Rosa Cándida Ramirez

"Common Ground: 3 Steps to Build Authentic Collaborations in Hard Spaces" by Bri Stensrud

"Beyond Multiethnic: Preparing Your Ministry to Faithfully and Respectfully Welcome Immigrant Communities" by Jeff Liou

# NOTES

## Session 2: Manifesto

[1]Laila Lalami, *Conditional Citizens: On Belonging in America*, (New York: Pantheon Books, 2020), 70.

[2]"Chinese Exclusion Act (1882)," National Archives, www.archives.gov/milestone-documents/chinese-exclusion-act.

[3]Becky Little, "The Violent History of the U.S.-Mexico Border," History.com, www.history.com/news/mexico-border-wall-military-facts.

## Session 4: Material

[1]"Migration as a Grace Conversation with Dr. Robert Chao Romero," Immigration Resource Center of San Gabriel Valley, https://ircsgv.org/blog/2021/2/9/migration-as-grace-a-conversation-with-dr-robert-chao-romero.

## Session 5: Motion

[1]Laila Lalami, "What Does it Take to 'Assimilate' in America?," *New York Times*, August 1, 2017, www.nytimes.com/2017/08/01/magazine/what-does-it-take-to-assimilate-in-america.html.

## Session 6: Closing

[1]"The Immigrants' Creed" by Jose Luis Casal, reprinted by permission from the Book of Common Worship, © 2018 Westminster John Knox Press. All rights reserved.

# MADE FOR PAX BIBLE STUDIES

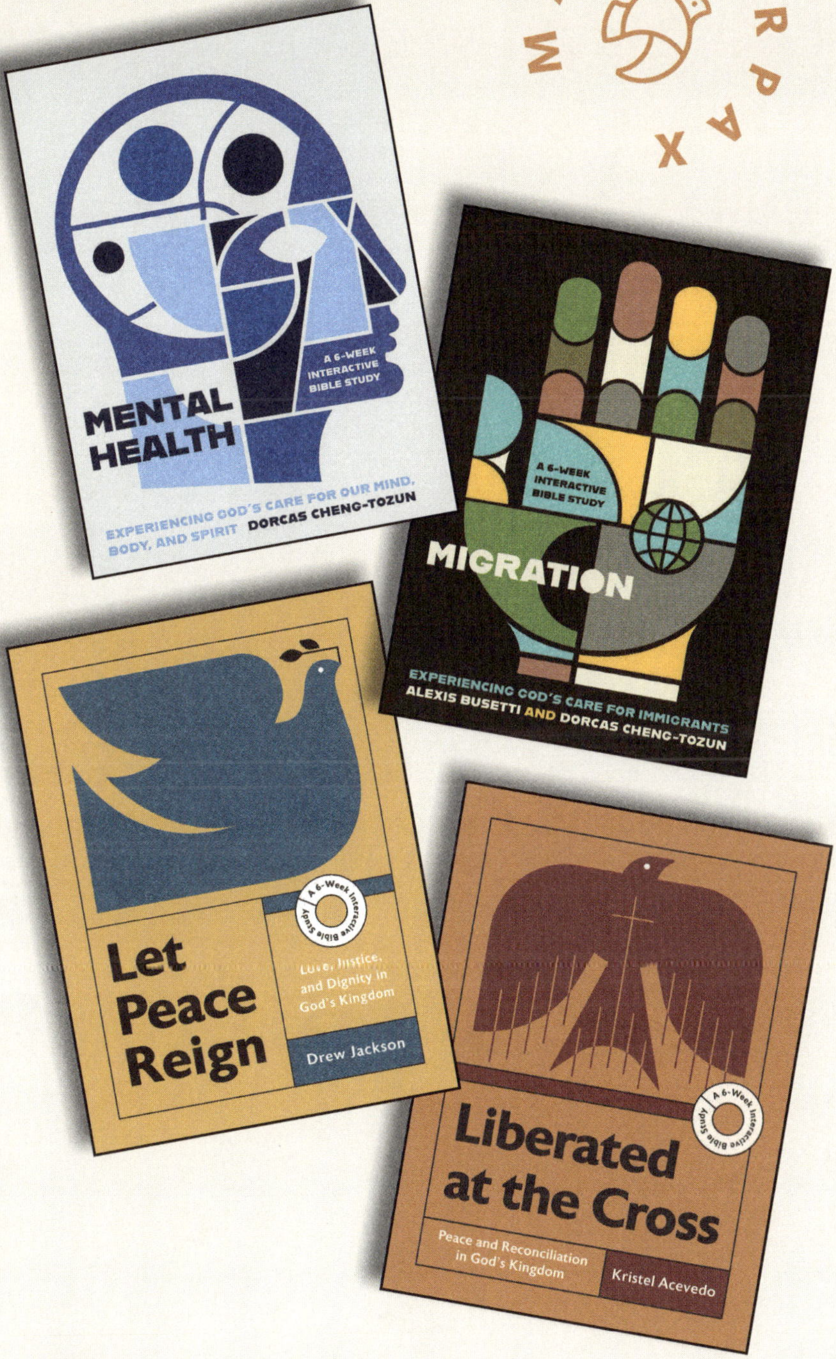


IVP Bible Studies

**ALSO AVAILABLE**
*Liberados en la cruz: Paz y reconciliación en el reino de Dios*

Made for PAX provides faith resources by Christians of color and empowers Christians of color through the PAX Fellowship, a nine-month program serving contemplatives, creatives, community builders, and church leaders at the intersection of peace, justice, and contemplation.

To learn more, visit ***www.madeforpax.org***.

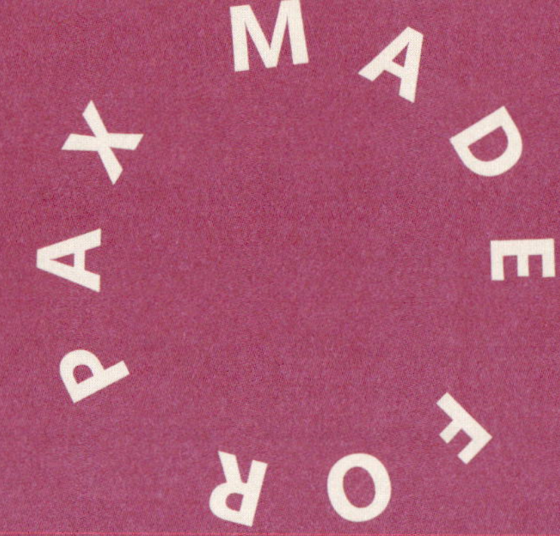
MADE FOR PAX